Precarity

Poems by Ian D Morris

Copyright: © Ian D Morris 2024

ISBN	Softcover	978-1-923021-16-7
	eBook	978-1-923021-17-4

All rights reserved. No part of this book may be reproduced or transmitted in any form or by any means, electronic, or mechanical, including photocopying, recording or by any information storage and retrieval system without the permission in writing by the copyright owner.

Cover Photo: Donieka Morris
Cover Design: Helen Brown

Published by: Reading Stones Publishing
Helen Brown & Wendy Wood
Woodwendy1982.wixsite.com/readingstones

For more copies contact the Publisher at:
Email: Readingstonespublishing@gmail.com
Or call 0422 577 663

Introduction, Dedication and Content Warning

Precarity: noun
- the state of not being safe or certain

This book is dedicated to all those who have, in some way, shared with me some of their experiences of trauma, loss and vulnerability.

There are many real-life stories woven into these poems. Stories of great challenge and great courage. There are no "true stories" in any sense of biography, but I hope I have been faithful to the truth of those real lives. As such, some of the poems in this book contain descriptions of, or references to, interpersonal violence and coercive control; suicide; war; and animal distress.

Please take care of yourself and seek assistance if you are impacted.

Ian D Morris

Foreword

First let me say how honoured I am to be asked to write a foreword to this unique and powerful collection of poems by my friend and respected colleague Ian Morris. Ian knows the subject he writes about well, having worked for a many years with people who suffer from trauma. This work is not for the faint-hearted.

Surviving trauma can separate us from ourselves. In trauma our amygdala (a small but powerful part of the brain) activates and equips our body to move speedily away from danger. Parts of the brain shut down, others rapidly mobilise, and natural chemicals are swiftly deployed around the body. The Marvel Comic Character, 'The Hulk' is a recognisable analogy to this. This process reduces our ability to think clearly, to control our emotions and bodies normally. This is ok, if the disruption is temporary and not overly impactful. Our brain and body return to normal when the threat has passed. However, if the trauma is regular or significantly impactful, this is a different matter.

In this state, colours, smells, anything that reminds our amygdala of earlier trauma can trigger a new episode in the absence of danger. Even if we don't remember the trauma, our body re-experiences it. This is PTSD, rendering us incapable of processing what happened and so unable to move on. Because of this we may start to mistrust themselves. Our uncharacteristic reactions may suggest to others that we are unreliable and so even supportive relationships become strained. If you would like to read more about trauma and its treatment, the bestseller "The Body Keeps the Score" by Professor Bessel van der Kolk, is a good start.

Trauma in childhood, may prevent the achievement of developmental milestones necessary for "normal" development. While others may say, "... that happened so long ago, haven't you gotten over that yet?" we may lack the foundations on which to build the normal strategies. For us to learn we must have the foundations on which to base new learning.

However, surviving trauma does not make us helpless or less than others. On the contrary, survivors are capable of amazing endurance, courage, intelligence and creativity, but they may enact it in unexpected ways.
I think this is why Ian wrote these pieces. Academic explanations of trauma pale in comparison to his poems, portraying the experience of trauma firsthand. Ian knows this because he and I both have had the absolute privilege of working with these incredibly brave and resilient people.

Nowhere in this volume will you find any betrayal of confidence or attempt to vicariously gain from another's misfortune. Ian tries to voice the unspeakable, to provide an echo for those who haven't been heard. Such is the power of poetry, and such is the tragedy of trauma. So please, for the sake of those who have experienced trauma, take these poems seriously and perhaps develop a greater understanding, but stay present. Vicarious trauma needs to be taken seriously. As Ian says in his introduction, please take care of yourself and seek assistance if you are impacted.

John Roy Wright- DipTch/EC, Bed, GradCertArts/Couns, M.Couns, Cert IV Train & Assess, Gold Key International Honour Society'

November- 2024

References:
1. Bessel van der Kolk, , 2014, The Body Keeps the Score: Brain, Mind, and Body in the Healing of Trauma, Viking Press,

Below are some of the Australian helplines:
blue knot helpline- call 1300 657 380. Information and support for people affected by complex trauma,
lifeline- 24/7 crisis counselling, call 13 11 14, or chat online. suicide call back service- call 1300 659 467. 24/7. Support for people who are feeling suicidal or are affected by suicide.

Contents

Precarity: a haiku	11
Monica	12
I remember my first day at school	13
Message to myself	14
Triggered.	15
One Big Red Tomato	16
This violent angst	17
Trauma and lament #2 (Lot's wife)	18
Precarity number 1	19
Institution	20
Kingdom	21
Dear Reverend John	22
The road re-travelled	23
Desolation	24
Precarity number 2	25
stripped bare of everything	26
the fine line	27
But they sent me flowers	28
Intangible Loss	29
Hidden in plain sight	30
Precarity number 3	31
Tiny	32
Don't let them take me back there	33
Our lives are predicated on the lives of others	34
Wait	36
Have you ever felt	37
Trauma and lament #1	38
Advice to a young therapist	39

Precarity: a haiku

all you need to do
is just believe in yourself.
i'm calling bullshit

Monica*
Greek: To give counsel, Alone.

Somewhere in the inner sanctum
of your memory
Coils a horror non-speak-able
And whatever words
that might have named it
have long since dissolved
in fear and shame
Leaving a hot knot of magma
To burn

And oh how it burns
In twisted guts
inexplicable aches,
The rashes
The scratches and
bruises in the night

In silence

Till even the kindest of doctors
Takes off her glasses
"There are no more tests we can do"

I remember my first day at school.

I remember my mother
in her seventies skirt
Pretty and kind

I remember the concrete step
and the room full of windows

I remember the teacher
Tall and safe

But mostly
I remember the ache

Message to myself

"Depression is anger turned inward." Dr Sigmund Freud, 1918

Take your life you piece of shit
And shove it where it fits
Take your moaning high horse
And flog it 'til it stinks

Take your aggressive assurance
And that shivering soul of yours
Take it to the Judas tree
I can't stand it any more

Take your ugly contentedness
That corpse of a narrow mind
Take your chains that no one wears
And walk a day in mine

Triggered.

The prettiest thing with her earbuds in
Walked her brand new pram
across at the lights.
The tradie in the truck saw his sister in
her hair flick.
He choked.
It wasn't her it never is.
He'd found her.
Purple and dripping shit.
His truck spluttered.
Crushing the steering wheel.
Her tattoo burned brutal on his scars
coughing up terror
to the sound of his offsider's wolf whistle.

One Big Red Tomato

From her window on the fifth floor
Sat back in the dark
Watching the war
Light up the night

Her head knew
She was far enough away to be safe
Her gut knew
Her babies would never feel safe again

How she longed to leave the light on
and ravage her man,
To dance on the roof with her friends
cheap wine and fairy lights
good music and bad hash

How long since she danced
How long since she put on that deep yellow dress
that made her skin glow
To wander the market for hours just to buy
one big red tomato

This violent angst

The lovers sat along the reach
feet in the water
to cool the heat
of visions of the dread.

Smoke still rising
from last night's bombing.
The toxic ooze of their
city's silent wound.

They hold each other
To hear their blood
scream this violent angst.

Trauma and lament #2
(Lot's wife)
After Genesis 19:1-26.

When he offered our daughters to the mob.
When the men who presumed to know told me
'you really don't want to see this'.
When we fled without the grandkids.
When he went ahead of me and never looked back.
When the bombs rained down and the ground opened up.
When the stench of burning flesh ripped through the streets
like ravenous ghosts.

I defy any mother to not look back.

I deny any father his redemption for not.

As my womb cracked open I rose up.
As my breast preserved in tears
I bore witness
to every woman and child in our city.

Precarity number 1

today was
full
so very full
the only breaks
were toilet escapes
that have a tension all their own

today was
another
scream of hours
minute squeezes
second gasps
time in labour

today has
died
may it rest in stress
and breathe a sigh of bitterness

Institution
(If we all left would it cease to exist?)

Inanimate frustrations
take on personifications
that incite me to rage
Facile policy
Faceless procedure

Who did this
Who ever thought
- This was ever a good idea
- Or adding that would help
- And the other thing was never going to harm

The powers become personal
The principality that feeds itself
The machine with lives
of its own
it's blood, cells and sinew
nothing less than lovely people
and me

Kingdom

what sort of god forsaken alchemy
is this
effigy of rag and bone
blood dripping like molasses
flies descending across time
the buzz
insidious as the smell
filling the space between belief
and everything else

Dear Reverend John

You inspired me a lot
but, in a way,
we were not friends.
And I admire you for not,
but I
have changed a lot since then.

The years have come and gone
like it seems,
they will not end.
And I've learned the right and wrong,
and seen
the faith in lesser men.

It seems a lot to lose,
but I feel
I'm on the mend.
But that does not excuse,
nor heal,
the bondage of religion.

The road re-travelled
"Seems like I been down this way before." Bob Dylan*

The tin man whips the lion
The straw man catching fire
Dorothy disappears
in a dungeon of daze

The monkey with a cotton eye
and a broken wing
Looks me up and down
with a soulless grin.

This ain't a nightmare son
It's the real thing.

---

*Dylan B (1978). *"Señor (Tales of Yankee Power) [song]"* Street Legal, Columbia Records.

Desolation

The night breaks like a fever
Limbs of stone crack under
Weight of sweat and stretch of breath
No soothing hum of traffic here
Even the crows have left
The light creeps in like cancer
Chest strains to contain the pain
Of the impossible scream

Precarity number 2

It never occurred to me to leave
I was too busy
managing everything for any
moment of false peace

It never occurred to me to leave
Until my youngest
asked if we could
I wept myself to sleep for a week until my guilted cage
flew open and we fled

I wish I could tell you life was good after that
We tried hard
It was hard
So very hard

The arguments with mum,
the 42 nights marked on the window of our car,
in and out of shelters,
schools, police stations,
years to get our own rental

My oldest got pregnant and left
'Anything is better than this.' she said
It broke my heart
to agree with her

We were wrong
so very wrong

stripped bare of everything

In memory of Sinead O'Connor 1966 - 2023

you cannot be forgiven for what you've forgotten
you can't steal a breath from the
dead

you misunderstood my tenderness
my screaming naked head
angels danced upon my lips
demons excised
from my chest

stripped you sit
on my death bed
the emperor's clothes
as your defence

the fine line

passed the night sign
along the fine line
between
sleep and dreams
dances
jesus on the sea of galilee
balances
satan's house and mortgage
swings
the pendulum of change
back and forth and back
along the fine line
between
sleep and madness

But they sent me flowers

When they messaged me a photo
From their blood-soaked bath

When they didn't stop
Wouldn't stop
Couldn't stop
Should've stopped

When the rules changed
Again and again
And again

And the stories changed
Should've changed
Could've changed
Would've changed

But they sent me flowers
Nothing changed
Again

Intangible Loss

Have you ever lost something
so intangible
that as far as anyone else is concerned
it never existed?

Have you ever lost a memory?

Have you ever lost something
that never was
because now it never will be?

Have you ever lost your mind?

Have you ever been obliterated
and no one noticed?

Hidden in plain sight

It's an in-obvious fact
that kindness and care
outweighs hate and harm
by ten thousand to one.
                        Or so they say.
That good people
outnumber the dangerous ones
by a vast percentage.

            Tell that to those who weren't killed
                that now wish they were.

It's an open secret that fear sells,
gets our attention, keeps us hooked.

                Yet fear is not harm itself.
                Fear is primal information.

It's a frightening possibility
that more of us are made sick by fear
than harmed by humans.

                Tell that to the mothers
                of the disappeared.

Precarity number 3

I only have my stories now.
Ghosts and diamonds
of my extra
ordinary life.

These young people
who come into my home
with their pretty uniforms
and sing song advice.
I don't understand what they want.

I don't know their stories.
They don't remember my stories,
or they don't believe them,
or they don't care.

I don't understand what they are saying.
I suppose it's that
I am old.
So very old.

But I have my neighbour.
She gives me yesterday's paper,
checks my mail,
calls my son.

I haven't seen her for months.

I only have my stories now.

Tiny

Marree lives in a commission flat
And has done for 30 years
Three floors up
and facing west
a tiny patio full of succulents

Marree loves her big cane chair
She found on the side of the road
Crocheted a cover
Took her a year
And it creaks like grandma's home

Marree has a gentleman friend
Visits every weekday but Thursday
Brings real milk
makes her Milo
And they watch the Bold and Beautiful

Marree has a big bed like grandma
Who always left a space on the left
Soft cushions
And plush toys
And a pillow of lavender scent

Marree has trouble sleeping
Though she always lays on the left
When the monsters come
her pillow she hugs
talks to grandma until they are gone

Don't let them take me back there

She pleaded to the trees
So trees told the soil
And the soil told the stones
And the stones told the mountain
And the mountain told the clouds
And the clouds told the sun
And the sun asked the universe to conspire

For one wonderous night
She escaped the monsters in her brain
And with the sunrise
She realised
The universe knew her name

Our lives are predicated on the lives of others

    cattle fowl sheep and swine
    left to their own devices
    build complex communities of collaboration

This we know.

    when cattle smell blood
    the frantic distress
    the poring ground
    the wild moaning bellows

This we know.

    i have looked the beast in the eyes
    to kill with a single shot
    to cut his throat
    to skin
    to slice
    gut
    and saw
    meat and bone
            and just like that
        we are talking about war
      starvation exploitation the poor
        protein power privilege
         predators that pray
         scar-city in-sanity
          rural suicide
           i'll decide

So what do we do now?

We do what any living thing does.

As if we didn't know.

Wait

The father wound is a grief
In whatever pathetic ugly meaningful way
it shows itself.

And fathers will kill time for it to heal.
I mean literally take time out the back and shoot it,
Starve it
of anything that might shake
its silent itch
its purulent weep
its deep chronic ache
its sheer terror
The father they had
The father they never had
The father they could be
The father they'll never be
The father they think they are.
The father their kids think they are.

The thing is
He doesn't know.

His father never told him.
He never told his father.

And so, he waits.

Have you ever felt

Have you ever felt
The blood sun
Rise up
Through the slum smog
Then the sedating heat
Soak up your every last will
To move

Have you ever felt alive.

Have you ever felt
Your heart beat
So loud
That the bed rocks
With the gun cracks
Holds your every last breath
Frozen

Have you ever felt alive

have you ever felt
dying eyes
look through
your shivering mask
into your soul
where God
could have been
where you left him

have you ever wished you felt alive

Trauma and lament #1

My heart is encrusted with years of unshed tears
In the cracks of this age
chunks break off into some kind of existential stroke

No mind can flush this fate free
No soul big enough
No body strong enough
No time long enough

So I howl into the dark
and rage and rage and rage

Somehow the darkness listens
This is where they all go
This is where we all know

Advice to a young therapist.

Aunty Jo looked me in the eye.
I know you are trying to help change his life.
I honour you for that, seriously I do.
We really do need more people
like you.

You are young and you have not suffered.
I see it in your eyes.
My brother here
has suffered.

I see it in his eyes,
in the way he sits down and looks around.
the way he eats his food and drinks his drinks.
the way of his walk.
I hear it in his talk.
What he says and what he
never says.

I pray you will never suffer like he does.
But he will never take you seriously
until he is sure you
understand the difficulties,
complexity and contradictions
of his life.

www.ingramcontent.com/pod-product-compliance
Lightning Source LLC
Chambersburg PA
CBHW030046100526
44590CB00011B/345